LEAVING LEGACIES

Breaking the Disconnect Between Parents and Millennials

Kovert Arts Publishing
McDonough, Ga.

LEAVING LEGACIES
Breaking the Disconnect Between Parents and Millennials

Leaving Legacies

Kovert Arts Publishing
McDonough, Ga.
www.kovertarts.com

ISBN: 978-0-692-67819-0
ISBN: 978-1-4951-9990-5 (electronic)

Cover Design & Interior Layout: Bryan K. Reed
bryankreed.com

Printed in the United States

Dedication

To Yaunte and Kayla Dvine, I lovingly dedicate this book to you both. I cherish my life with you two and look forward to our legacies carrying on.

Godspeed.

Table of Contents

Acknowledgements

I would like to acknowledge all the people below for being a reliable community connection and for supporting my belief in healthy mental living and family safeguarding.

Bayyinah Shaheed, Owner of The Parenting is Prevention curriculum
www.besmartdontstartbesmartquit.org

Michelle Watson, Editor and Owner of Topflight Communication
www.1topflightcomm.com

Bryan K. Reed, Freelance Designer
www.bryankreed.com

Kandi Conda, Hall of Famer/Speaker/Author/Entrepreneur
www.kcbizboss.com

Introduction

This book is designed to increase the knowledge of parents, giving them new ways of thinking and new options for parenting their children. Its purpose is to increase awareness for parents and their children related to family unity and personal communication patterns. Many of today's parents grew up in homes in which yelling, cursing, hitting, and belittling were common forms of parenting. They not only adopted their parents' methods, but have added calling the local authorities, having school hearings, and juvenile probation to what will be part of their children's memories of growing up. In the following pages we will discuss these maladaptive reaction patterns and provide tools to decrease the generational disconnection they cause, and teach parents to create an environment of family unity. Though the word "parent" is used throughout the book, these tools are applicable for anyone who is the primary caregiver and support of a child from the millennial generation (anyone born in 1990 or later).

I wrote this book out of my concern for parents and their children. In my practice, I counsel families on a regular basis. Many of these parents come to me with children who have been labeled "bad," "disruptive," or ADHD. There are many medical and biological reasons children may have adjustment problems or have trouble sitting still in school. However, many of the problems that make children "act out" and seem undisciplined can be improved with the communication and family structure guidelines that I have developed after nearly a decade of counseling parents and families.

Read through the book and do the thinking exercises that will help you reflect on your own parenting style and the influence your parents' child rearing methods have on your own methods. More importantly, consider whether your parents' methods were effective. Did they bring you closer to them, or push you away? Did you grow up angry and bitter towards your parents, or do you still love them and seek to truly honor them? Knowing the answers to these questions will help you understand why your child rearing methods may or may not be effective with your own children. For your convenience I have included a Family Meeting Guide at the back of the book. Use this information to have more productive family discussions. By including your children in the discussion, and not just talking at or to them, you will give your family a mentally healthier environment and make the entire home seem less stressful. To further aid in your self-discovery as a parent and to build positive communication between you and your children, visit the web address provided in the Family Meeting Guide to download the thought-provoking two-page worksheet.

Part I

Communication Patterns and Parenting Styles

Communication Patterns

Communication - the human connection - is the key to personal and career success.
Paul J. Meyer

Communication patterns impact the family in positive and negative ways. Researchers claim 90% of communication is nonverbal. We tend to define nonverbal communication as body language, but it really is so much more. Nonverbal communication includes tone, inflection, and the look on a person's face. Parents become unaware of their own body language and perceived attitudes, and forget their children are watching their every move. Do your children mimic you when they are on their cellular devices or other gadgets? Have you ever asked yourself if your children were modeling your behavior correctly? If so, are they modeling behaviors you wish to have tvhem learn? Children are always watching their parents and attempting to imitate them. Without even speaking to parents, their children can immediately identify thoughts connected with anger because of their parents' physical appearance, like frowning, clinched fists, or a change in vocal tone (yelling, gritting your teeth), etc. The mental and emotional impact of negative communication from parents towards children can improve when parents become more aware of new ways to create positive verbal and nonverbal language patterns.

Even answering a question can send a nonverbal message to a child. Too many parents are questioned by their children when directed to simply put on their coats and prepare to leave. Parents feel defied, but children simply view the situation as parents not understanding them. "I was only asking a question," says the child. Parents often become irritated due to constant questioning (back to back) from their children, "Where are we going? How long will it take? Who is going to be there? Do I have to go? How long are we staying?" As many parents know, these questions are irrelevant and don't always warrant answers. However, many parents find themselves answering these sorts of questions one after the other until they become irritated and begin yelling out of anger and frustration. The child's perception remains, "I was only asking a question," while they then blame the parent for being upset and having a bad moment without accepting any responsibility for their own behavior. Many families of this millennium engage in this circular, dysfunctional dialogue on a consistent basis, which ultimately aids in destroying the family unit. Many children of this generation (1990 up) haven't been taught how to engage in a meaningful conversation, but rather how to talk just to hear themselves speak (how some parents describe excessive, pointless conversation or "talking back" behavior of children).

So, let's discuss the previous example in which a child's questions were referred to as having no purpose. Part of parenting is directing and guiding children to help them grow and mature into responsible productive citizens of their community. Parents are required to be responsible for the safety of and accountable for their children to avoid legal issues in connection with negligence or abandonment. In turn, being questioned by a child becomes irrelevant due to the fact that the parent is parenting at that time! Children have to be taught how to have meaningful questions and conversations; this is done by parents being aware of their own verbal and nonverbal communication with their children. Parents should question themselves on how they react to their children's defiance and challenging behaviors. When parents become conscious of how they react to their children, it leads to the children having more purposeful thoughts and displaying desired positive behaviors. Once they are consciously aware of negative habitual reactions, parents can choose to change that reaction and react in a positive, consistent manner.

Examples of positive manners include: Remaining silent; not being quick to answer children when they ask meaningless questions (take time to quietly ponder the relevance of the question so you can be purposeful in your answer). Avoiding behaviors like yelling, belittling, and striking (just to name a few negative behaviors) due to feelings of frustration and being annoyed at not feeling in control of the conversation with the child. Taking the time after questioning sessions from your children to explain to them how their questions are unwarranted and how clarity and comprehension works. Use this prime opportunity for quality bonding between parent and child and to reinforce values and morals, expressing how excessive talking may socially impact them as well.

My Story

"The older you get the dumber your ass gets!" were the words I heard on a regular basis.

I began to believe as a teen that the older I got the dumber I was getting. This belief was embedded by my father each time I missed the point of a moral lesson or life lesson that he wanted me to learn. I eventually learned from my mistakes but became fearful of repeating the behaviors that caused him to call me dumb. The older I got, the dumber I became. I later came to understand, that what I was being told at critical stages of learning in my life were in fact lies. As my efforts to further my education continued to advance, so did my feelings of self-worth.

Now, back in the 1970's and 1980's, this form of negative communication (belittling) was "normal" among families from various backgrounds and ethnicities, not to the extent of child abuse, but a form of punishment just the same. Feelings of low self-esteem and negative self-worth were ingrained through a strong environment of negative reinforcement. Such mental conditioning increases the risk that an individual's decision-making abilities will become and continually be irrational. It was common to hear parents calling their children something other than the name they had legally given to them, out of anger, frustration, or simple annoyance.

Aggressive Communication

Aggressive communication is defined as someone expressing personal needs and desires without thinking of the welfare of others (Cuncic, 2016). See, each time I was told I was getting dumber as I was getting older, my emotional welfare wasn't being considered. My father never considered whether I was starting to believe his philosophy or the impact it would have on my self-worth as an adult. Also, at those times my father would give direction or commands in a purely dictatorial manner, which left no room for compromising or negotiating. Even though my father's parenting style reflected much of the aggressive communication style, I never felt that his desire was to hurt me or seek out revenge against me, which are both core characteristics of aggressive communication (intentional hurt and revenge). But, his form of communicating was an open door for poor emotional development to occur, which is a common result for those on the receiving end of aggressive communication. Aggressive communication often includes blaming, name-calling, rationalizing, and minimizing situations to favor one's self. Some parents may use an aggressive communication pattern more often than they realize. When parents respond to their children with such examples as I have listed below they are setting the tone for aggressive communication patterns to begin.

"Because I said so." "You never…" "Do as I say, not as I do." "I brought you in this world and I will take you out!" "Ain't nobody gonna come in my house and tell me what to do." "You're just like your…" "Why are you acting stupid?" "Dumb Ass!" These were all phrases commonly heard from parents in my neighborhood in the 1970's and 1980's. Parents thought they were getting their children to really think about their behavior. In fact, just the opposite was true because children tend to internalize such aggression and believe they, not their behaviors, are the problem.

Parents must be mindful of passive communication as well, as it is another form of aggressive communication, just less verbal. When parents use this form of communicating they are able to avoid conflicts with their children. However, parents are soon left with feelings of depression, anxiety and helplessness. Children may take on feelings of frustration and anger because of the disconnect caused by the lack of ability to communicate with their parents because the parents themselves are not mentally or emotionally present to communicate. It is important to remember the negative emotional impact that aggressive communication has on children, and that it decreases their chances of success.

My Story

I have already told you about my father's aggressive style, but he was not the only one. And, unfortunately, the other adults in my life left much deeper scars in the way they communicated.

My elders were all very strict when it came to how children were to talk with adults. No tolerance was given for talking back, pouting faces, stomping feet, or leaving while being spoken to. This left an impression on me far into adulthood. When I became an adult, I was fearful of talking back to another adult, even though I was one! It felt weird and wrong to correct an adult, even if I knew they were wrong and I had the facts to back me up.

I would quietly sit back and allow an "elder" to speak to me with horrible disrespect just because they were older than I and it was instilled in me from childhood not to talk back and to allow the elder to have the last word. As I continued to grow older and wiser, I began to understand that age doesn't matter because right is right and wrong is wrong. I had to make a decision to learn how to communicate better to save myself. I even found myself crying and sad when I allowed an elder adult to question my intelligence, belittle me, and talk down to me just because I wouldn't do what she wanted me to do. I had decided to stand up for myself and express my feelings to her based on how she was making me feel. I had learned to use assertive communication to counter her aggressive communication. I will address assertive communication in the next section.

Needless to say, this changed the direction of my relationship with this particular elder. So much changed that we haven't spoken in years. My elder—my step-grandmother—used words that cut me like fire after the passing of my mother. She didn't approve of the handling of the funeral services and felt that I should have paid for more and done more when, in actuality, my stepfather was in full control. Her communication to me was emotionally deadly to me—an adult, mother, wife, and entrepreneur—making me feel worthless over something I couldn't control. I had to change how I communicated to save myself, and to teach self-respect to my own daughter.

Assertive Communication

Most of the parents I encounter from the Baby Boomer Generation and from Generation X have struggled with using assertive communication because it not only requires more talking, but also requires parents be open to their own feelings of self. The benefit of assertive communication is that it allows people to express their desires, thoughts, needs, and feelings in a straightforward, open manner. An assertive communicator is concerned about the welfare of self and others because everyone is important in the conversation.

In order to implement assertive communication parents must be willing to commit to a change in lifestyle by forming new habits. Assertive communication is effective when speaking with children and adolescents, as well as in other relationships. This style of communicating is most effective when practiced consistently. When applied to parenting, assertive communication causes parents to focus on responding to their children instead of reacting to them. Parents must use assertive communication to verbalize to their children how they truly feel about situations and circumstances honestly, without being hostile, speaking loudly, blaming, belittling, using profanity, etc.

An example of someone utilizing assertive communication is, "I don't like it when you yell at me. It scares me. Can you please talk in a lower tone instead?" In this example, the speaker is stating how they feel when someone does an identified behavior, and the speaker then gives a suggestion on a better way to communicate for them to engage. Let's look at another one.

"I don't like it when your teachers call the house to complain about your talking back to them. It makes me feel embarrassed. I will set up a conference with the teacher so we can all talk face to face."

To utilize assertive communication, the speakers have to focus on themselves following this format, prior to reacting to the person who has upset them. The steps for parents to follow are:

1. Identify the problem, the behavior, or trigger that is making the parents feel upset.
2. Express a true feeling related to the problem or circumstances. This is crucial because at this point parents are teaching their children how to express their feelings with words in the form of positive communication. Children now have the opportunity to hear how feelings other than sad, mad, and happy are expressed by the parents who have the essential task of guiding them through life.
3. After verbally expressing their feelings, parents have the option to explain why they feel this way. This step is optional, and taking the time to explain can easily mislead children to believe that their parents' feelings related to the situation are open for discussion. Explaining at a later time may help parents reiterate the importance of why the child should discontinue the behavior. (Refer to the Family Meeting section of the book to learn ways to explain situations or decisions to your children based on morals and how to spend effective, quality time with your children.)

4. Lastly, when using assertive communication, parents must inform children of what they would like for the children to do instead of the identified behavior. Parents should use this time to brainstorm with children other ways to react instead. Taking time to brainstorm with children on other ways to behave helps them widen their knowledge of the possibilities that are available to communicate in a positive manner. A good thing for parents to practice is to teach children how to implement assertive communication for themselves.

My Story

I had heard aggressive communication at home and on the streets of Detroit, but, I knew I could do better. I didn't have to live as a victim of aggressive communicators, and I didn't have to be like them, either. I did learn, though, how to stand up for myself by being assertive.

I used to experience a rollercoaster of emotions when the phone would ring in the 1990's, fearing it would be a bill collector. Having dealt with aggressive communicators in my family, one would think I was ready to take on bill collectors. And, I was. Before I understood how to manage my finances, I would get calls all the time from bill collectors. I was already naturally angry and frustrated at not having the money to pay them, so when they called and used their bullying collections tactics on me, I would yell and scream at them. This got me nowhere with them; it only escalated the problem, as any collector I spoke with would surely call again and the cycle would continue—I couldn't pay, they would call and get belligerent, I would yell back at them, and it would all happen again the next day. It wasn't that I wanted to argue with people or avoid paying my bills; but I really needed to address the fact that even strangers were communicating aggressively with me. I had begun to mimic the aggressive communication I had learned from others. This why it is so important for parents to understand that everything they do, or don't do, communicates with their children and teaches them how to behave as adults. Don't fall into the trap of believing children will "do as you say, not as you do."

Now that I know how to manage money and have better mental clarity concerning both my finances and good communication techniques, I don't get calls from collectors anymore. However, when the occasion does occur that requires I speak with an accounts receivable department about a bill I owe, I am able to implement assertive communication. Due to my perception of my business with a certain company, I can calmly explain my feelings, my thoughts, and the desired outcome. This allows me to easily make arrangements to handle the account and my business with that company.

Something to think about:

* Do you know the communication style you use most often when communicating with others?

*What would the two people closest to you say your communication style is if they were asked?

PARENTING STYLES

At the end of the day, the most overwhelming key to a child's success is the positive involvement of parents.
Jane D. Hull

Now let's talk about the different parenting styles since we have a better understanding of communication styles. Before we go any further just guess which style you use the most and which one your parents used.

1. Authoritarian Parenting
2. Authoritative Parenting
3. Permissive Parenting
4. Uninvolved Parent

You use ____________________ Your parents used________________________

Okay. Now let's see if you are right!

Authoritarian Parenting

Authoritarian parenting is a style in which the parent doesn't leave options open for discussion. "My way or no way" is basically how authoritarian parents operate. Children are expected to follow orders without questioning or talking back, unless they want swift repercussions. Children who are subjected to this form of parenting style are not responsible for independent problem solving, or adapting to and overcoming obstacles or challenges they may face throughout their day. This style of parenting can cause children to rebel and display mischievous behaviors as they continue to develop. The parents also may consider themselves being "strict" or "old school," referring to how they were raised or how their parents were raised back in the 1950's through 1970's. Children with authoritarian parents are rarely given reasons for the rules that are established by the parent and there is little to no room for negotiating or compromising on the stated rules. Children of this millennium lack understanding of how to build healthy relationships with others due to their parents' attempts to control and shape their children to meet their standards of "absolute."

Authoritarian parents may not be considering the impact of the decision-making process and the ability to understand the power of "choice" during the stages of childhood development. This form of parenting takes away the child's ability to believe in self in regards to choices they make in relationships. This negative interaction will carry over into the teenage and adolescent years of dating and further, on into adult relationships. Middle and high school students' relationships are enhanced today due to school attendance, which increases interactions with others besides parents for longer periods of time. Additionally, technology and social media offer children the ability to connect to strangers instantly. The dichotic messages children receive between their parents and the rest of the real and online world is very stressful for them. The desire to become independent as they get older will cause them to listen to their friends at school and their online connections in rebellion to the authoritarian parent.

Authoritarian parenting does have a positive impact on long-term compliance, by following rules set by authority figures. However, the negative impact is that it tends to hinder self-esteem from childhood to adulthood. They are often more withdrawn and anxious, and have unhappy dispositions, even after they become adults. Children of authoritarian parents tend to become angrier with or more hostile towards others (mainly parents and authority figures) due to living with reprimands or punishments, instead of being taught to form their thoughts into confident decisions. When faced with the challenge of making a decision or solving conflicts independently the child is more likely to display acts of poor self-esteem, self-doubt, and impulsiveness. These children have been trained to do what is instructed in the presence of their parents, but have trouble when parents are not present to provide good decision-making skills. Parents often hear complaints about their children's behavior from the school and the community (church, YMCA, summer programs, neighbors, etc.), such as disrupting class, talking back, not following directions, playing excessively, etc. Authoritarian parenting is a forceful style of parenting, with the desired outcome of forcing children to cooperate with the parents' desired command, and when parents (the force) are no longer around children will act on their own will. This style leaves children with physical, spiritual, emotional, and mental damage over time as they continue to develop.

Authoritative Parenting

Authoritative parenting describes parents who establish rules and guidelines their children are expected to follow. However, it is much more democratic than authoritarian parenting. Children expect structure and guidance from their parents, and are looking for ways to assist their parents in establishing the system. Children feel safe, secure, and loved when given reasonable boundaries by an authoritative parent. The authoritative parent's rules are considered age-appropriate and realistic for both the parent to enforce and the child to adhere to because they are set with respect for the viewpoint of the child. Parents are able to set rules that are not based on emotions, but on clear, concise thoughts that add value to the family as a whole.

Authoritative parents are responsive to their children, willing to listen to their children's questions, and are interested in their children's daily activities. They are mentally aware of a child's self will and the connection between discipline and obedience. Authoritative parents are also mindful of the importance of fostering children's individuality and self-regulation. These parents are more nurturing and forgiving in their disciplinary methods, rather than punitive. They are assertive, but not intrusive and restrictive. Such parents have the ability to avoid parent-child conflicts by focusing on family goals, because children are more open to taking direction from a positive authority figure when they feel they are purposeful in the world. Children become open to finding solutions when they develop a higher level of self-confidence. Rules are not just given, but explained to children to help them see the value of having to establish each rule. Positive consequences and praise for actions are more prevalent in authoritative parenting.

Children who have authoritative parents tend to be happy and successful in life throughout middle and high school because they learn to set the goals they want to strive to accomplish. They are able to display good decision-making and problem-solving skills and typically grow up to be responsible adults who are able to verbally express their thoughts and opinions. Involving children in decision-making situations related to home and family creates a sense of unity in them, and bonds children and parents together. Authoritative parents put more emphasis on home and family life. Both major and minor decisions include both the children and the parents, not just the parents, giving children a true sense of purpose and belongingness. Authoritative parenting is the ideal parenting style because children learn to place value on their lives, and they develop the ability to express their emotions appropriately, no matter whom they interact with. Positive communication and praise for good behavior are more prevalent with authoritative parenting than with the other three styles.

Permissive Parenting

Parents who routinely do for children what they could do for themselves (i.e., cleaning their rooms, preparing their food, doing their laundry, etc.) are classified as permissive parents. This behavior labels parents as enablers due to their inability to set clear guidelines for their children as they develop into adults. Permissive parents typically don't set standards for children to adhere to, but instead allow the children to set household rules and guidelines. The permissive parent is more agreeable and accepting of the child's behavior instead of shaping values and desired behaviors in their children. When children display negative impulses, actions, or undesired behaviors, permissive parents are more likely to blame others for the child's actions, as opposed to holding their children accountable and searching for areas where they could improve their parenting strategies.

Permissive parents struggle with being their children's role models for the long-term benefits it brings versus being their children's friend for the short-term peace it offers. Children of permissive parents then place themselves in a position of control and will consistently engage in verbal power-struggles with their parents. These parents make few demands and fail to establish order in the home, which causes children to disobey authority figures outside the home (at school and in the community). We see examples of permissive parents all the time. They are the parents who negotiate and reason with a child in the store rather than simply telling the child "no" and letting that answer stand. Children who are not made to understand "no means no" often throw tantrums, storm off, or become loud and demanding. These children are looking for inconsistency in the parenting leadership so they can control the situation's outcome. More unfortunate, though, is that such children are actually controlling their parents. As the children of permissive parents become adults, their self-esteem and self-confidence are negatively impacted due to the missed opportunities to learn life lessons they should learn during childhood. Life lessons that should be learned in healthy ways from failures are lost due to parents' hindering their children from experiencing hurtful emotions. For example, disappointment, embarrassment, shock, and desperation, are all things a child should experience and learn from if allowed to develop naturally.

Another common trait for the permissive parenting style is what is called the "helicopter parent." Helicopter parents tend to "hover" over their children and are often extremely overprotective. Consistently overprotected children tend to become very needy and do not socialize well with age-appropriate peers. Discipline and structure are not important factors to permissive parents. They often only become involved when a serious issue arises, such as a court case or problems at school. However, they are still extremely lenient when it comes time to instill punishments or consequences for misbehaving and poor decision-making. These parents are often told things like, "You need to be the parent, and not their friend," as friends and family judging their parenting style as more of a friendship relationship (focused on gaining acceptance) instead of a parenting relationship (focused on establishing values and morals). The children are allowed to talk about their feelings and emotions openly but with no insight as to how their thoughts direct their paths in life or how they are able to alter undesired situations by their own behaviors.

Parents who use the permissive style of parenting may, at times, allow their children to take control of the parenting aspect of their lives in an attempt to keep the children from acting out. Children may, in turn, become antisocial, unruly, disruptive, and unable to complete tasks in a timely manner. Most children will have severe emotional regulation issues with permissive parenting. They may also be labeled with mental health diagnoses like Oppositional Defiant Disorder, Attention Deficit and Hyperactivity Disorder, or Conduct Disorder.

If you realize you have been an authoritarian or permissive parent, you may need to enlist the help of a licensed professional counselor, a parenting group, or parenting aid classes to decrease your risk for family disconnect.

Do Any of the Following Sound Familiar?

1. "It's not fair!"
2. "You love [sibling, spouse, etc.] more than me!"
3. "I hate school."
4. "So, I don't care."
5. "You never listen to me."
6. "You never let me go anywhere with my friends."
7. "You're not my real parent."
8. *"I'm gonna kill myself – someone else – or hurt you."
9. "I am not going to take my medicine."

10. "I just lie."

Many parents rethink their decisions based on being told that they are not fair by their children. This type of response from a child is rightfully considered disrespectful and defiant by authority figures and school officials. But, in an effort to not "play favorites," being called "unfair" causes many parents to relent on their rules and consequences. A parent's willingness to relent indicates a power struggle is occurring. The power struggles between the parents and the children often result in explosive outburst/melt-downs either by the parent or from the child. Parents must be mindful that this is sometimes a distraction method used by children in an attempt to get what they want after being told "no." Parents must hold their ground when setting rules and consequences and avoid feelings of guilt or thoughts of being provoked after hearing that they are not being fair and so on. Parents can join parenting support groups where they can ask questions and seek guidance on the latest parenting tips. Family counseling and individual counseling services are available through many local facilities and private practices.

*Please note number 8 from the above list. It is extremely serious and should be taken so. Parents must contact 911 and seek professional help immediately. Parents should also be aware that children sometimes use the threat of hurting themselves as a way to persuade parents to alter their perspective on a particular issue, with no real intentions of harming themselves or anyone else. Even still, any time these threats are made, parents should closely monitor the child and seek professional help immediately.

Uninvolved Parent

It is easy to recognize the uninvolved parent as it relates to single moms and "deadbeat dads." However, some would say there has been an increase in single dads and "deadbeat moms" since the new millennium. Many fathers today accept the responsibility of full custody of their children while many mothers pay child support and receive visitation rights. The truth is, ”uninvolved parenting” can just as easily happen with two parents living under the same roof as their children.

Uninvolved parents can be physically present in their children’s lives, but abandon them spiritually, mentally and emotionally. For example, a child witnesses a parent participating in spiritual rituals such as going to church, reading the Bible, praying publicly, and so on, but never includes the child. Uninvolved parents never give their children the authority to determine if they would like to participate. They don’t take the time to simply explain the purpose of church and why it is of value to their family and their lives.

One familiar statement from uninvolved parents is, “You don’t think before you act,” which children mentally interpret as I am incapable of thinking logically for myself. Although, physically, children are able to see and touch their parents, their parents’ aggressive communication style creates a mental wall. Children then develop feelings of being hurt, not belonging (lack of closeness), and feeling as if they are not good enough, which fuels the discord in the family unit.

Many times children struggle to find their identities due to living in a two-home family because of separation or divorce. This causes increased anxiety in the children as well as the parents. Both parents and children are transitioning to a new life, which brings challenges, rewards and uncertainty, with bottled up feelings of anger and frustration. Often, absent parents do not focus on the actual parenting process, but instead on the relationship they may have had with the custodial parent. This always becomes an emotional and stressful experience for the parent and the child to overcome. Parenting styles sometimes change with mood swings, placing both parents and children in stages of emotional distress. For example, an uninvolved, divorced parent (father) attempting to offer guidance (encourage male camaraderie and toughness in his absence) may tell his son not to smile in pictures. The son, attempting to honor his father, is then scolded by his mother for not smiling. The conflicting parenting style from the uninvolved parent and the custodial parent often triggers non-compliant behaviors and feelings of anger for both parents and children. Discord increases in the family dynamic and tends to rise to the point of causing one parent to become estranged or altogether gone. Children can easily identify their parents' inability to co-parent, and many times begin to suffer in school with a drop in academics and peer relations, and attach to negative social influences (gangs and inappropriate social apps). They may develop low self-esteem and have little to no understanding of self-worth.

Going back to the parent coined as "deadbeat," which is a common way of referring to a parent's financial contributions, or lack thereof, to their children. Deadbeat parents tend to never provide emotional, mental or spiritual support for the child, which leads to precarious parental supervision. Meaning, even if the children physically see the absent parent, they still don't feel spiritually, mentally or emotionally secure in the presence of the parent. Whether this form of parenting is referred to as uninvolved, ghost, absent, or deadbeat parenting, it is typically associated with neglectful parenting and requires parenting aid classes, parenting groups, and/or family therapy to divert family disconnect.

Uninvolved parenting fosters a lack of discipline and a lack of developing moral judgment because the parent does not take interest in their child's desires or needs. Communication channels are typically nonexistent because the uninvolved parent does not establish stability in the child's life.

When I was a young girl there was a commercial that would play every night at 9 p.m. on television. The announcer would ask, "Do you know where your child is?" Uninvolved parents who are ghost or absent don't know where their children are, or what their children are doing.

Quality Praise

Be kind whenever possible. It is always possible.
Dalai Lama

Sometimes it is hard to show appreciation to children for displaying positive behaviors unexpectedly. Sometimes, when they uncharacteristically follow directions, it may be hard to thank them. Why? Well, when children have behavioral problems, like failing to follow directions from authority figures, intentionally annoying others, stealing or lying, etc., the level of frustration that parents endure becomes heightened to the point that parents can become emotionally disconnected from their children. A parent may, out of desperation find themselves pushing a child away by not participating in quality activities like eating together, praying together, going to the nail salon, the mall, the skate park, or fishing, etc., which ultimately increases the disconnect in the family unit and fuels animosity, lack of cooperation, secrecy, and distrust. Many parents' lifestyles are impacted financially, emotionally, and spiritually because of children with behavioral issues. They may face the loss of a job and being shunned by family and friends. Over time, parents begin to limit emotional, financial, and spiritual support to a misbehaving child due to their inner frustrations from parenting a child who is constantly a cause of unplanned school meetings and legal issues that cost time, money, and mental sanity.

Some parents justify forgetting about using manners themselves because they are not consciously trying to be a role model in a particular moment. This is a LIE. It is NEVER okay to display improper adult behavior with children or other adults. Treat others as you want to be treated, right? The truth of the matter is that it is key to thank children and show them impromptu moments of gratitude for their small, sometimes tiny, positive behaviors. Below are the steps to a quality praise exercise. It will help get you in the habit of observing moments of your child's good behavior and actions. This exercise of giving praise needs to be separate from the big occasions. Although you may see a need to acknowledge your child's good deed on a major holiday or during a birthday celebration, these celebrations cannot take the place of the quality praise exercise.

The quality praise exercise goes like this:

Step 1: Wait until your child is not paying attention to you and is carrying on normal, daily activities (maybe washing dishes, eating diner, preparing to go to bed, etc). Notice the child doing something (action or behavior) that is right.

Step 2: While the child is minding their own business walk up to them and casually place your hand on their shoulder. Look them in the eyes and verbally acknowledge the positive behavior you have witnessed. It may have been helping a sibling get some water without complaining or putting the garbage in the can instead of on the floor after eating candy. It may be something "simple" that you as the parent noticed in the past but never acknowledged.

This also works by calling the child to you. After noticing the positive action displayed by the child, call the child's name as you normally would. Command them to come to you, "Angela, please, come here." Expect the child to talk back by questioning you or intentionally not answering you. You are calling them for the purpose of completing this exercise; don't allow yourself to respond to the child's talking back behavior. Instead, wait 3 to 5 seconds, then repeat your instructions. Continue until the child is in arm's reach.

Step 3: Hold your child's hand, arm, or shoulder while staring into their eyes thanking them for the action you just witnessed them complete. At this moment you are only awaiting acknowledgment from them that they understand your praise for that particular "simple" behavior.

Step 4: Once your "thank you" is acknowledged, drop the mic! Instruct the child to carry on about their business prior to your interrupting. Do not have a conversation with the child for any reason. They then must leave your presence and continue with their prior task. The importance of this step is to have the child bask in the positive reinforcement they received from you related to their behavior.

Small moments of gratitude to consider:

1. When you notice the child is sitting correctly at the dinner table
2. When the child assists a sibling with getting water without complaints
3. When the child does what was asked (chore) on first prompt without talking back
4. When the child says something positive about someone else
5. When the child stops after being told on first prompt
6. When the child doesn't have to be reminded to complete a chore
7. When the child says a proper greeting when entering the room
8. When the child tells the truth
9. When the child states something positive about themselves
10. When the child looks others in the eyes when speaking
11. When the child shows compassion for others
12. When the child says "yes" instead of "yeah"

Bonus When a child's response shows that they have thought prior to speaking

Many times parents who have children with defiant behaviors find themselves only verbalizing their children's' negative behavior when speaking of their children to others. This is a dangerous habit that has to be broken. As a parent, become more determined to communicate positively, not just verbally but physically, emotionally, and spiritually with any children who have been marked as disruptive, unruly, disrespectful, juvenile, delinquent, etc. It can increase their chances of erasing that label and living a more positively guided life. The key is that you must be purposely mindful of how you are interacting with your child each time you are together. Now it's time to learn how to guide your child and to be mindfully purposeful in your interactions.

You MUST display such polite behaviors as:

1. Saying "thank you," "please," and "you're welcome"
2. Cleaning up after yourself
3. Demonstrating how not to interrupt and to wait your turn
4. Males must hold doors for females, or the younger female for the older female
5. Not saying hurtful things
6. Demonstrating proper driving etiquette
7. Using proper phone etiquette
8. Listening to others when they are speaking
9. Saying "May I…?" and "Excuse me"
10. Offering your seat to elders
11. Giving firm handshakes
12. Showing consideration for guests
13. Demonstrating good table manners

More than likely you grew up with structure, limits, and boundaries that were enforced with something as simple as a squinting stare from across the room from your parents or grandparents (really, anyone who was older than you). That squinting stare meant action was sure to come if a certain behavior didn't cease immediately. Whether it was a tug on the ear, a pinch on the arm, a pinch on the shoulder, or a pop with a comb, something was coming for continued defiant behavior (it was not yelling and verbal threats that a lot of parents—especially young ones—mistake for discipline). For the majority of today's children, this method of grabbing a child's attention doesn't work, and instead creates power struggles between the child and the adult.

Parents today need to actually practice new ways to grab the attention of their children, ways that command respect and order. Children are longing to be validated and reassured that they belong to someone or something. Understanding the magnitude of the right word at the right moment can connect a parent and child with the feelings of support and unity. When we want to show approval, we praise others.

Quality praise shows a parent's approval to a child in a way that is intentionally purposeful. It will increase the child's level of self-esteem and help them believe they can do "something" right and that their parents actually notice. Implementing this technique takes dedication and commitment from parents to become more aware of the positive behaviors child does daily, although the exercise is not intended to be used daily. This method of parenting allows parents the opportunity to emotionally connect with their teenagers or children in a positive manner that is unexpected for the children. It physically draws the two individuals to each other through physical contact (hand on shoulder or holding hands) and looking into one another's eyes. Teachers of all grade levels who teach children with behavioral issues or students who have been labeled as disruptive, "bad," or defiant can also implement this exercise.

The goal is for the family unit to have positive interactions between all members in order to communicate effectively and to complete the family mission (leaving legacies). Each family member must know how to give and receive praise. The point is to thank the child/teenager for minor task completions such as getting clothes ready for bed, putting the keys in the proper place, holding the door, etc., for the sole purpose of reminding the child that they are able to do "good." Quality praise is never to be given with a sarcastic undertone or a negative intent. This is NOT the time to bring correction on how something was done.

Poor communication patterns in the home between parents and children are consistent with the lack of positive reinforcement. Parents often find themselves withdrawn emotionally from their children due to repeated negative incidents that impact the family as a whole as well as the family unit members individually. Implementing these four steps to quality praise may help improve the self-esteem of children who have found themselves being labeled at home, at school, and in the community as juveniles, unruly, disruptive, etc., and could ultimately decrease impulsive and unwanted behaviors.

Embracing Parenting and Social Media

It's hard to think of any tool, any instrument, any object in history with which so many developed so close a relationship so quickly as we have with our phones.
Nancy Gibbs

Do you know what the popular web addresses are for social media?

There are unlimited numbers of inappropriate internet sites within the reach of children, and that's why it is imperative that parents stay in tune with technology and what their children are knowledgeable of when it comes to social media sites. There are some social applications that clearly identify what ages the content is appropriate for. However, the ultimate responsibility belongs to the individual using the site, or parents, when the user is a minor. If parents are not providing supervision as it relates to the use of technology then, of course, curiosity will get the better of a child. It is good to question your teens related to their likes and dislikes of the apps that are available to them and designed for them. In doing so, you may redirect them to a more productive community on a more positive social platform.

Here is a list of some of the apps used on smart phones, iPads, computers, laptops, etc.:

Twitter	Flicker
Instagram	Snapchat
Google+	Kik
Pinterest	Ask.fm
LinkedIn	Periscope
Meet.me	Blab.im
Classmates	Twitch.tv
Meetup	Anchor.fm
Vine	Facebook

It is unrealistic to believe that children are not going to be exposed to one or more of these sites or apps beginning in grade school (elementary). Even if children are home-schooled, they may still be subjected to seeing these sites because of the socialization that surrounds teens today, fulfilling the instant gratification this generation starves for. Millennials desire instant connection, and when they are not feeling satisfied in the home, the internet is the next best, albeit virtual, world. The internet continues to be a proven trap that has been the cause of numerous traumatic events such as murder, suicide, running away, illegal sexual behaviors, etc. Parents must embrace social media and acquire a solid understanding of it to communicate properly to their children the rules related to social media, explain how to handle online bullying, and the importance of unity within the family as a whole.

Here are some apps that are designed for children that have parental control:

Club Penguin
GeckoLife
Help Your Hero
Franktown Rocks
BeSean
Kimingo
PlayKids Talk
Kidzworld
Sweety High
iTwixie

Let's look at some of those with less parental control a little more closely…

Texting Apps

Kik Messenger-Alternative texting service that lets teenagers **chat and swap pictures** while **bypassing the wireless provider's SMS service**. This means the device doesn't have to be turned on in order for the teen to use the phone's internet access. There is no fee to use this app, which is the main reason it is popular among teens. This app allows unlimited messaging and character limits for users and group chatting abilities. **Allows children to text strangers!!** Kik also has a community where users can share screenshots of their messages and images of themselves. This app has been linked to crimes, including a 13-year-old girl who was allegedly killed by an 18-year-old male she met on Kik. ("Kik messenger app scrutinized after 13-year-old's death", 2016).

WhatsApp – This app comes with unlimited messaging and no fees, designed for users **16 and over**. The users are able to send photos, text messages, videos, and audio messages. Parents should be aware that their children are active on this site as well. Supervision should never be taken for granted; children/teens need guidance.

Ask.FM – This app is allows the **user to ask questions**. Many teens like using this app unsupervised; it is full of sexually explicit questions and online bullying questions. The internet is full of stories that share how teens have taken their lives because of relentless cyber bullying and negative peer pressure. Properly monitor teens by knowing their friends and by showing models of healthy relationships to help teens avoid having feelings of low self-esteem.

Small Blogging Apps and Sites

Instagram App – This is a popular app in which users are able to take 15-second videos (with editing ability) and pictures with options of showing in private or public view. Popular to many teens because of the "Like" feature in which they attempt to boost their views by leaving location on, or including #hashtags that are popular at the time.

Twitter App – This is a networking system that feeds information on the latest world and local news related to subjects that the user has interest in. When a user sends out a message it's referred to as a "tweet," with each tweet being limited to a length of 140 characters. Normally, tweets are sent out publicly, but the user has the option to send private tweets, and each tweet posts immediately. **Even after a user deletes a tweet it is still there for followers to view**.

Tumblr – More characters than Twitter's 140 are allowed for messaging with this streaming scrapbook of texts, photos, or videos and audio clips. The short blogs are called "tumblelogs." This online hangout may contain **pornographic** images; supervision should be present if a teen is using this site.

Vine – This app has endless loops of **six-second videos** of everything from babies crawling to teens dancing to the newest hits. But, it also demonstrates just how much porn one can pack into six seconds. Teens are drawn to the creation of making videos of themselves, friends, and families.

Video Apps

Snapchat – Another popular app for teens because it allows users to share **photos and videos** that are programmed to automatically **self-destruct in 10 seconds** or less. Teens use this to make videos of what they are doing when bullying others and displaying inappropriate sexual behaviors.

ChatRoulette – this site lets **anyone engage in video chat via webcam** with random strangers. Similar apps include Omegle, Chat Random, or Dirty Roulette.

ooVoo – This app allows users to send text messages, audio messages, videos, and photos to one or more people with no message limit or fees. Up to **12 people** can be on the chats at one time. This app only allows you to chat with **approved friends**, making it safer for teens to socialize without talking to strangers.

Chatting, Meeting, Dating apps

Tinder – A "**hookup**" app, Tinder allows users to scroll through images of other members and flag the ones they like. **FYI: Tinder's minimum age is 13, and it is very popular with young adults in their early and mid 20s!!** This is a messaging app with the purpose of meeting in person as the goal. It is location-based, so parents must be aware of the location features on this and all other apps. Parents must have rules in place that they communicate to their teens related to their safety and the family's safety.

Calculator Plus – This is a free app that teens place on their phones, and parents have no clue of the misleading dangers. The app is not only for calculations of mathematics, but of secrets. Upon entering a numerical pass code the app opens up and turns into a storage space where teens store inappropriate photos of themselves and others.

Texting

Texting is apocalyptic on some level. It's a reduction of things.
Nick Cave

Texting is another form of communication widely used by adults and children and, sadly, used too much between parents and millenials in order to communicate. Texting is a shorthand version of typing, primarily for cell phones, though it is also used on other technological devices. It is the fastest way for millennials to communicate, and they have created their own language just for texting. Parents should be aware of how their children are using cell phones to communicate by understanding the shorthand language being used. Try to decipher the message below.

AT&T posted an advertisement that warns parents about the need to know their children's texting language and to be involved in their teens' lives.

Do you know what mnE Ps dnt b-lev der is a d/c b/t dem n der teen iow mnE teens KPC means? (2006)

The translation is "Many parents don't believe there is a disconnect between them and their teens, in other words, many teens keep parents clueless."

Understanding Text Messages

Here are some common terms parents should be aware of when reading text messages. A good practice is to ask teens regularly what the latest text language is. Be mindful of texting others when communicating in general. Question the comments and texts and ask for clarification. Use the internet as a search engine to learn the latest text language and apps.

- **TTYL** - talk to you later
- **WYD** - what you doing
- **IDK/ION** - I don't know
- **IGTG** - I got to go
- **TMI** - Too much information
- **SMD** - suck my di*k
- **POS** - parents over shoulder
- **IWSN** - I want sex now
- **420** - marijuana
- **9** - parent watching
- **99** - parent gone
- **8 or 69** - oral sex
- **KPC** - Keep parents clueless
- **THOT** - That "hoe" over there
- **TDTM** - Talk dirty to me
- **WTTP** - Want to trade pictures
- **Cake** - Booty
- **SUGARPIC** - Suggestive or erotic picture
- **LMAO** - laugh my ass off
- **PIR** - parent in room
- **POV** - Point Of View
- **SH** - Sh** Happens
- **SOL** - Sh** Out of Luck
- **RBTL** - Read Between The Lines
- **Beat** - Beautiful
- **DM** - direct message
- **Fleet** - Looks good
- **IOW** - in other words
- **4SHO** - For sure
- **DKFS** - Don't know for sure
- **FASHO** - For sure

- **FO SHO** - For sure
- **FO'Shizzle** - For sure
- **INS** - I'm not sure
- **GNOC** - Get naked on camera
- **NIFOC** - Naked in front of the camera
- **IPN** - I'm posting naked
- **GYPO** - Get your pants off
- **JMS** - Just making sure
- **LMIRL** - Let's meet in real life

Part II

Family Meetings

Family Meetings

Family is not an important thing. It's everything.
Michael J. Fox

Many parents struggle to find a connection with their children. The bond between parent and child is too often barely noticeable, or it's full of anger and sarcasm. Many parents seek ways to improve their relationships with their children in an effort to decrease the disconnect. Parents openly admit that they sometimes shut down on (withdraw from) their children due frustration over defiant behaviors. Many times parents are not able to recall the last time they spent quality time with a child, or when they last had a purposeful talk. Quality time is the key to building and reconnecting parents with their children. If parents make the effort to pause their busy schedules and actually spend time with their children (without distractions) they will see a drastic, positive change in their relationships with their children. However, quality time must be consistent and purposeful. Parents who are able to give consistent and purposeful quality time to their children are more able to have the desired relationship with their children, one that includes happiness and a fulfilling connection.

The value of holding family meetings is to create a sense of belongingness (verbally and non-verbally) between all family members. When family meetings are held consistently, family members begin to connect emotionally and intimately. Family meetings allow each family member to talk out their thoughts and to be heard without judgment. The structure of the meetings allows for the family to make decisions in unison, and creates an environment where each person can feel good about their growth in life as a family unit and as individuals. Primary topics covered in the meetings should be based on morals and values delivered through encouraging, inspirational, motivational, and educational messages. Families need to be open and vulnerable with each other to avoid detachment from others and the realities of their lives. Without emotional security, the families become dysfunctional, which is a primary cause of the increase in juvenile offenses and why unruly behaviors persist.

The head of the family (identified parent or other head of household) must gather all family members together to explain to them that there will be routine family meetings each week. When the family gathers, they should begin the meeting by ensuring that all distractions are removed and by demanding the family's undivided attention (eliminate cell phones, television, radio, etc.) during the gathering. The parent should pick a time in which each family member can attend the gathering, such as bed time (prior to bed, call all children to the kitchen), dinnertime (make each child sit at the table for a special announcement), or just after arriving home. Notice I didn't say in the car, or while the parent is cooking, because this exercise has to be accomplished face to face. It is important to maintain eye contact as much as possible when explaining the changes you expect in behavioral patterns (setting family structure). The parent should give the day, time and length of the meeting to take place at some future point. The rules of the meeting should also be explained at this time, such as no blaming, name calling, or negative statements are to be used during the meeting, and any other rules related to the family meeting (see Family Meeting Tool). Parents should hold the gatherings within three or four days of informing the family of the meeting to come. Allow the family members time to adjust to the concept that quality family time has been planned, and it must remain positive. Then stick to your word!

Vision

Where there is no vision, there is no hope.
George Washington Carver

Let me begin this chapter by asking you a question: We make plans and have visions in other areas of our lives, so why not do the same for our families? When you are creating your family vision, dream big. Don't just plan for one goal, but several, and dream up everything possible for every member of your family unit. When we do not have a vision, we cannot accomplish our mission for our family, and therefore fail to plan for our family's success. Success is spending quality time together, teaching your children how to read social cues in different environments, and promoting your children to express themselves through talents and gifts that build their self-esteem and confidence. Dreams of important things, like instilling in your children that they will go to college, start early by your talking about higher education and preparing your children at a very early age. Let children know that attending college IS a possibility for their future. When you tell children from birth that they will go to college, they tend to believe it and live as if they know they are going to college. If you want your family to be more unified and cohesive then you have to begin by envisioning it, and by planning how that vision can be reality for your family.

The problem is that today some, if not all, family members' thoughts are centered on their smart phones, computers, and iPods, etc., with no thoughts being placed on meaningful family interaction that is without a negative overtone. Often, parents are trying to maintain a day-to-day workflow and keep up with the latest gadgets, fashion, and social media trends. Their children mimic this behavior, finding themselves spending more time with electronic items and peers, hindering the personal emotional connection needed for the family to be a healthy family unit. Too often, families are divided and disconnected due to a lack of focus on the family as a whole. Having an agreed on, family-centered vision will help everyone feel connected and less reliant on their cell phones and gadgets to replace the love and togetherness of family.

People gripe and complain repeatedly about the fact that one can't plan everything. Yet, in order to complete a task as simple as brushing your teeth, you must plan it. Moving through life is a plan that everyone has. However, everyone doesn't attempt to organize their journey as they are moving. When you're moving through life and you're not sure of what the next level is, you may experience feelings of frustration and being overwhelmed. Successful people (whether financially, emotionally, mentally, or spiritually) plan their days, months, and years. It's not that they know for sure what each day will bring or what they will accomplish day to day, but successful people prepare for what they want in their lives. They envision the items, objects, and platforms for their lives, and they work in a direction that is in alignment with the journey they see for themselves. They organize their thoughts related to making their visions and journeys come to fruition, understanding that it will not come without failures and moments of disappointment and despair.

Due to lack of vision in families today, adolescents are on individual paths, where their primary thoughts are related to what they want for themselves. They have little to no compassion for others. Their smart phones, computers, tablets, etc. are programming their minds, and they put no conscious thought into positive family social interactions. Children view family social interaction in a nonchalant, carefree manner because there is no unity within the family. Prior to the millennial era, parents only had to worry about television interfering with their parenting methods from the outside. Now, social media provides instant connection to outside interferences that many times override parents' rules and guidelines, destroying the family unit by blurring the family's vision. Many parents find themselves teaching their children negative habits by displaying behaviors that are inconsistent with the words they speak related to what they see for themselves as parents and for the family as a whole.

For example, the vision begins to become blurred when the child is being ridiculed or yelled at for interrupting the parent while the parent is viewing social media accounts. The reaction of the parent may encourage negative feelings within the child, in which the child could perceive the ridicule or yelling as lack of value for their thoughts and feelings. Such thoughts could ultimately lead to the child's mimicking of the parent's reactions to others, including the parent, thus creating a disconnect between the two. Hence, no family vision.

Successful entrepreneurs take time out of their day to organize their thoughts for their employees so they can complete a productive workday. This is done while juggling their home activities so they can manage their families (feed children, clean) and prepare for the next workday. Successful thinkers also take time to think about the purpose they are serving in life, what is purposeful to themselves as well as to their families. So, planning is an essential part of breaking barriers of poor communication patterns for families and decreasing family dysfunction. Success requires planning for ups and downs as the journey of life is traveled. The plan that brings your family's success will be determined by your vision and the steps needed to reach your goal.

So, planning is an essential part of living a successful and purposeful life. Therefore, it should be incorporated in families' as well as individuals' daily living styles, and with conscious intent. A good tool to help in breaking barriers of poor communication patterns for families and decreasing family dysfunction is to identify the family's vision. Plan your vision; write it out, including how the family can accomplish it. Make a vision board so the entire family has a picture representing the vision, making it more tangible to all the family members. When planning out your family's vision, don't be surprised if something comes up that is not in your plan, but that requires your immediate attention. Expect good things to come up that are not written out in the plan, and expect bad things to come up, too. That is all a part of the vision coming to pass. The vision for the family sets the direction for all family members to consciously see and speak on. So, when negative moments happen in your family's life, address them and brainstorm ways to stay on course for the vision. Use setbacks as opportunities to learn and grow, and to enhance your opportunities to communicate; don't let them become excuses to give up on the vision.

Making a Family Vision Board

When constructing your family vision board, utilize tools such as a poster board, decorative paper, markers, pictures, magazines, and fabric. Anything you want to use is fine, as long as the family works on it together and the items that go on the board represent the family's agreed-upon vision. If you find your family's ideal home in a neighborhood 30 minutes away, let one of the children take a picture of the home to put on your vision board. Same thing if you find the ideal family car. You may even go to the car dealership and get a booklet of your family's dream car, cut it out, and paste it on the board. Make sure each family member helps and all their thoughts are considered rather than deciding what is ideal for the family on your own just because you are the parent. Once all the items for the vision board are in place, hang it in a place where it is only visible for the family members it represents. It should not be hung in a collective gathering area where extended family members and friends have easy access to it. This vision board is NOT a conversation piece for others; it s a conversation piece for the family unit it was created for (parents—or caregiver—and children of the exclusive family unit).

Family Mission

A mission statement is not something you write overnight... But fundamentally, your mission statement becomes your constitution, the solid expression of your vision and values. It becomes the criterion by which you measure everything else in your life.
Stephen Covey

There are three components to family missions

1. Input
2. Realistic Goals
3. Action

According to Merriam-Webster's online dictionary, a "mission" is defined as "a body of persons sent to perform a service or carry on an activity" (2015).

A family mission should include input from the primary parent(s) as well as from each member of the family. The purpose is to set the tone of how the family works together to accomplish end goals that will help each member of the family individually and the family as a whole in the future in some way. For instance, the parent may have a vision for the family to become free of generational poverty, defined as two or more generations of a family that has survived in low economic circumstances (Urban Ventures, 2015).

In this example, the parent will demonstrate leadership by gathering input from all family members related to their thoughts of ending the poverty lifestyle. Next, the parent gives guidance by making realistic goals that are in alignment with the overarching goal of ending generational poverty. Finally, the parent informs the family to take action, which creates a sense of unity and belongingness, thus motivating the family. The mission has now begun, as each member begins to move in ways that fulfill the identified goals. Parents must get out of the habit of thinking they should not share the burden of the cost of living with their teenagers because their parents didn't share such information with them. Many parents recall how they felt when their parents spent money on purchasing new items such as cars, boats, designer shoes, and so on, instead of explaining about what monies were being spent and why.

Any parents attempting to escape generational poverty need to allow the family to be a part of the decision making, or at least informed of the decisions, as they impact each member as a whole. Millennial children must be heard, unlike teens of past generations who took on the belief that children have no voice when it comes to their thoughts and feelings related to the family's decision-making process. For today's teens it is very valuable for the family unit as a whole to allow them opportunities to verbally express their feelings and thoughts related to the family business. Allowing teens to verbalize their emotions related to the family unit validates their existence in the family structure, giving them a sense of purpose within the unit. Ultimately, the parent(s) must do what is best for the family, but allowing the children (particularly teenagers) to verbally express their thoughts and feelings related to the changes in the family's direction is crucial to decreasing family conflicts.

Parents trying to overcome the pattern of generational poverty will talk with the family members about why they are no longer paying for internet at home, or why they are not paying for cable, for instance. They will glorify the fact that they've chosen to put their money in a savings account or checking account that will allow them to make a future investment within three to five years on a new home. The parent and family will then celebrate the vision of property ownership for their generation and the next. Mission is on!

Be aware of negative comments from others when setting your mission into action! When parents establish a vision for their children, it sets them apart from other family members who may not have a vision for their immediate family. But the parents with a vision have begun programming their offspring to think in a more financially sound way as well, if we use the example provided of a family ending generational poverty. Parents who are able to appreciate delayed gratification, to focus on the value of long-term outcomes, and to think of sacrificing now for the pay-off later will catapult their children into financial wealth and diminish the cycle of generational poverty that has kept their family in a poor economic status for years.

Getting every family member's input is going to require QUALITY time being spent with each member. Their input is something that cannot be gathered in one day, but it will be done over time. Once the goals are identified, more quality time will be needed with each family member to successfully complete the mission.

Goals

A family's mission must have a **realistic goal** to be accomplished. When speaking of a realistic goal, the goal should be attainable with the able bodies and minds of the people who make up these outcome-driven goals. Parents should have realistic steps and objectives that each family member can carry out. They should ensure that their values and ideas are in alignment with the family's desired goal. Parents should verbalize the point that one day the family will have their own home and not reside with others based on the behaviors that the family will take every day, week, and year. These steps should be centered on mental, physical, emotional, and spiritual paths for the family as they embrace the transition of a new mindset that will end generational poverty.

When parents are attempting to create goals, objectives, and interventions, here are some things to keep in mind. A goal is established because it has an identified outcome. When setting goals a parent should know when the goal is accomplished because an end has come about or a desired change has occurred. For instance, a goal could be that Jenny would stop throwing objects when told to stop touching things that don't belong to her. This goal will be accomplished when Jenny is able to perform a different behavior immediately upon being told by an authority figure to stop touching things that are not hers, as opposed to throwing whatever Jenny touches. The next thing to keep in mind is that objectives are the steps that a person can actually do over time that are directly related to changing the undesirable behaviors and learn new ways to deal with the events and/or situations. Finally, parents are to put in place interventions that are both external and internal support systems to help the child overcome barriers and obstacles that hinder the child's progress. Parents must look at goals, objectives, and interventions in ways to help establish the family mission and move the family forward.

Many times children are in a hurry and catch parents off guard. Both the child and the parent must STOP, literally, and treat every word with thought. Having the ability to use patience prior to responding to each other can increase the pathway to the family vision. The habits of reacting quickly are part of the habits that may have helped the family in the example above continue to remain in poverty. Understanding the importance of implementing new behavioral patterns when engaging with each other can provide clarity in the family vision as the family continues their journey. This will require parents to avoid moments of shutting down and avoiding interaction with their children. It will also require moments when each family member consciously decides to remain silent and purposely avoid responding with an argumentative tone. The value of the family system will begin to define the traits and characteristics for each member to uphold as the family continues to verbally communicate in a way that is related to the mission they are collectively on and their accomplishments.

Action

In the paragraphs above, in the section on goals, you read about interventions. Action is where the interventions come to life and the actions you take as family will take you on your journey to changed behaviors. I saw a post on Facebook once that read, "First they will laugh, then they will copy. Don't give up" (Motivationblog.org).

Parents have to be the leaders in the family who are willing to stand up for the vision against all outsiders. STAND UP because once you have a vision for your family, the "Naysayers" and the "Why-ers" are going to come out in full force. Let me clarify a little about these people I like to refer to as Naysayers and Why-ers. These are the people who have the same family members as you, and some are your closest friends. They are co-workers and friends you grew up with, they are church members who think "their" God couldn't have given you your vision. They are boyfriends and girlfriends who believe if you start the mission and complete the vision you will no longer want or need them. They are bosses and peers, and sometimes your spouse or your children. All these people have the same thing in common: they don't believe in your vision. They don't see your dream. Guess what? They are not supposed to, because it's yours, NOT theirs. You must beware of these people when you start to take action on the mission because they will make you change your mind, second guess your thoughts, and dismiss any actions that you dreamt of doing. They will have a mountain of information on why you can't achieve your goals, why you can't achieve your vision. They will challenge your every move towards your goals with questions about why you did this, why you said that, why you did it that way, and why you are thinking like that.

The family members on the mission will be taking action together. From each day to each week they will have conversations related to breaking the behavior patterns that have been holding the family hostage in the mindset of the generational poverty cycle (or hostage from completing any other goals they set). Each word the family speaks related to breaking the behavior patterns connected with generational poverty (overcoming any barriers or obstacles) must be in the form of positive communication for effective teamwork, thereby creating action. Family meetings with conversations discussing methods to climb out of economic hardship are essential for taking action towards the mission. Telling the Naysayers and the Why-ers that you don't have time for their negative commentaries about your family vision is also action. Teaching your children to be mindful of the Naysayers and Why-ers, as well as how to respond to them, is taking action. Educating yourself and your family on ways to spend and save money is taking action if your goal is to end generational poverty.

The process of developing a family vision is to get TIRED, yes, become tired of the same day to day existence that is inevitably leading the family nowhere positive no time soon. Find the desire to LIVE, not just EXIST! When this happens the vision is formed. In order to have a vision you have to DREAM; you must think of the FUTURE. When your days are not improving and begin turning from days into weeks that become years, and you realize that you are in the same situation financially, physically, mentally, emotionally, and spiritually, and others around you have left, moved on, and achieved more…dream it could be you, and your vision is born.

Erik H. Erikson

Erik H. Erikson was a developmental psychologist and psychoanalyst who passed away in 1994 (Erik Erikson, 2016). Have you ever heard of someone having an "identity crisis?" He developed the theory of the psychosocial development of human beings and that phrase was coined after his work. He was able to identify eight stages of psychosocial development, starting with infancy. He believed that humans' personality development begins through a series of identity crises. It is important to review his stages to help parents grasp a better understanding on what crisis issues their children may experience as they develop and mature. Each stage has been broken down into three categories: crisis, potential (new virtue) and societal manifestation.

Stage 1 0-1 years of age
In this stage children develop a sense of trust when parents provide reliability, care, and affection. A lack of these components leads to mistrust. The child begins learning all about "hope" and "faith" at this stage, unless mistrust is formed. The primary activity is feeding.

Stage 2 1-6 years of age
Toddlers and preschool-aged children need to develop a sense of personal control over physical skills and a sense of independence. New physical skills lead to demand for more choices, most often seen as saying "no" to parents, or to anyone, really. Success leads to feelings of autonomy; failure results in feelings of shame and doubt. The power of "will" is being established at this stage. Primary activity is toilet training.

Stage 3 6-10 years of age
In this stage, children begin asserting control and power over their environment, which results in a sense of "purpose." They have the ability to organize activities around some goal at this point. Children who try to exert too much

power experience disapproval, resulting in a sense of guilt. Primary activity is exploration.

Stage 4 10 to 14 years of age
Children in this stage need to cope with new social and academic demands. The "competence" with cultural skills and norms, including academic skills, are now what the child should be mastering. Too much criticism of their work at this stage can lead to long-term feelings of inferiority. Primary activity is school.

Stage 5 14 to 20 years of age
Teenagers at this stage need to develop a sense of self and personal identity. The adolescent needs a unified and consistent sense of self that integrates pubertal changes into a mature sexual identity. They are able to assume adult social and occupational roles and they begin to establish personal values and attitudes. Failure in this area of development leads to role confusion and a weak sense of self. Think of this as when teenagers are trying to develop their own separate identity while "fitting in" with their friends. Primary activity is socializing.

Stage 6 20 – 35 years of age
Now, intimacy "love" is important. Young adults need to form intimate, loving relationships with other people. These relationships are more than "puppy love" or adolescent love; many of the young adults become parents. Young adults who are secure in their own identity can proceed to an intimate partnership at this stage, but the isolated person may have affairs or even a long-term relationship, but always avoid true closeness. Primary activity is forming relationships.

Stage 7 35 – 65 years of age
Adults need to nurture or create things that will outlast them, often by having children or creating a positive change that benefits other people (living a "productive" life). In this stage of development, thoughts are centered on rearing

children, focusing on occupational achievement or creativity, and training the next generation with a focus on caring for others. Adults who are successful in this stage develop feelings of usefulness and accomplishment, while failure results in shallow involvement in the world. Adults who are not successful in this stage become stagnated and absorbed in the past. Primary activities are working and/or parenthood.

Stage 8 65 plus

At this point in development, older adults need to look back on life and feel a sense of fulfillment. The person conducts a review of their life in which they integrate earlier stages and come to terms with their basic identity, which they develop into a sense of self-acceptance. Basically, some people look back and accept the good and the bad while others have nothing but regrets. Success at this stage leads to feelings of wisdom, while failure results in regret, bitterness, or despair. Primary activity is reflecting on life.

Erikson's eight stages of the cycle of life are (Erikson's Stages, 2016):

Age	**Stage**	**Crisis**	**Potential**	**Society Manifestation**
0-1	Infancy	Trust vs. Basic Mistrust	Hope	Religion and Faith
1-6	Early Childhood	Autonomy vs. Shame & Doubt	Will	Law and Order
6-10	Play Age	Initiative vs. Guilt	Purpose	Economics
10-14	School Age	Industry vs. Inferiority	Competence	Technology
14-20	Adolescence	Identity vs. Role Confusion	Fidelity	Ideology
20-35	Young adulthood	Intimacy vs. Isolation	Love	Ethics
35-65	Maturity	Generativity vs. Stagnation	Care	Education, Art, & Science
65+	Old Age Ego	Integrity vs. Despair	Wisdom	All Major Cultural Institutions

RULES

"Love recognizes no barriers. It jumps hurdles, leaps fences, penetrates walls to arrive at its destination full of hope."
-Maya Angelou

When it comes to rules, the most common complaint from parents of millennials today is that they are very disrespectful. To parents, disrespect comes in many variations: smoking weed, skipping school, failing grades, claiming gang relations, interacting with older men/women, being sexually active, fighting, threatening assault, using profanity towards parents and other authorities, disobedience, and poor self-care to name a few. In addition to these challenges, we must now include the negative influences of corporate marketing and socialization.

According to an article published by Marketing-schools.org, parents and children become "influenced by every message, jingle, logo, billboard, and celebrity spokesperson associated with a corporation" (Corporate Marketing, 2012). We have all experienced that one song that won't leave us alone after hearing it on the way out the door in the morning, a prime example of marketing doing its job. The article went on to say that "even when consumers aren't paying attention, the message remains in their field of consciousness, or their peripheral vision" (Corporate Marketing, 2012). Negative corporate marketing and socializing influences can directly connect with children through tools such as social media, magazines, etc., by way of tablets, cell phones, computers, and other electronics. As hard as parents try to forbid their children from using such tools to interact with others, the marketing is impossible to avoid. The world in this generation is designed to stay connected with free Wi-Fi, free live streaming, low-cost payment plans for gadgets, and the list goes on. Even prisoners are able to make videos and post them to the internet with contraband cell phones (Evans, 2015). The likelihood of parents' preventing their children from accessing social media at will is not very high. But, hope for our young millennials can be restored!

How do you begin to establish rules or structure for children who are unruly and lost in the social movement of social media?

One of the biggest challenges in parenting is sticking to set limits and boundaries with children who are non-compliant and who become hostile at any given minute. Some parents attempt to establish rules and structure but fail to follow through with the consequences, or the child is simply disobedient. When disciplining young millennials, many parents fail to understand that continuing with the parenting styles of the 1960's and 1970's (screaming, yelling and hitting) as discipline will only continue to generate negative results. Parents' behavior patterns have to be re-evaluated. Many times family and friends have already evaluated, commented on, and verbally corrected a parent's disciplining techniques, but because of the continued negative behavior of the child, the parent struggles to change their own repeated patterns. The ability to follow rules is an important element for children in developing integrity and character. As early as the toddler years, children should begin to be disciplined, because without rules from an authority figure they become lost (misguided and confused). Children who are made to follow systems are able to socialize appropriately (teamwork, sharing, getting along with others, etc.) and become more productive and successfully independent in their adult years. The belief system instilled in children is based on their parents' morals and values and their ability to manage life's stresses. Without having consistent rules that are fair and age-appropriate the children and parents will begin, or continue on, a journey of frustration and anger that ultimately results in an extreme disconnect in their relationship. No legacy is left.

When parents think of setting rules for unruly young millennials to follow, it is only natural to think of the resistance that children give with the mere thought of being told what to do. Today's parents have to also consider new external factors such as social media, corporate marketing, etc., and how they impact our parenting styles when setting rules. Wi-Fi, electronics, and repeated negative behavior, or the escalation of negative behavior, are common areas of complaint when millennial parents are questioned about their frustrations with parenting. Unsupervised, Wi-Fi can be a thorn in a lot of millennial parents' sides due to the instant connection and the availability of access. Parents must stop supplying their children with the newest version of cell phones, tablets, gaming systems, MP3 players, computers, and all other electronics without setting interaction limits and boundaries. When asked, a majority of parents report that they take all electronic gadgets from their children as a form of punishment or discipline. Eighty percent of the parents questioned stated that they rarely give their child a timeframe for when the punishment will be over. The stress of managing multiple children, full-time work, single parenting, or poor marriages were some of the reasons parents stated for not being able to follow through on the rules they set. Seventy-five percent of parents reported they continue to add to punishments they set when a child continues to misbehave. The reality of this generation is that their social movement is social media, so taking them away from social media actually increases the broken communication between the young millennial and the parent.

Parents must embrace electronics and Wi-Fi and introduce these devices to their children by explaining their expectations and limits for these gadgets. Parents can decrease their children's outbursts over the loss of their electronics when parents have to take them away. First, though, parents have to stop abruptly removing the gadgets solely because they have the authority, or because they purchased the item. It is imperative that parents implement supervision when distributing devices that connect their children to social media and not simply give these devices to their children. Devices must be given with accompanying stipulations, rules, limits, and boundaries.

When children begin to escalate negative behavior, or when parents continue to witness repeated negative behavior patterns, that's a good time to re-evaluate oneself as a parent. A parent's reaction to a child's behavior often can influence any further reactions from the child. Many times millennial parents are unaware of their own responses until it results in an explosive situation that requires a third party to diffuse, or when it has brought harm to the family unit. Distraught parents should seek professional mental health providers as an option, not family members, friends, or social media.

When it is time to instill punishments a good concept to consider is the S.M.A.R.T. method. S.M.A.R.T. stands for: specific, moral, attainable, realistic, and time-limited. S.M.A.R.T. is a great method to implement when deciding on the rules, rewards, and punishments for your family. The point of implementing the S.M.A.R.T. thought process is to increase moral awareness in the children and their parents by decreasing poor communication patterns. Many children are not sure about how to safely express their concerns and feelings when it comes to socializing in the world of social media or verbalizing their perception of corporate marketing. Parents do not regularly talk with their children about the dangers of society. Again, this lack of communication leads to an increase in family conflict and disconnect. Implementing the S.M.A.R.T. way of thinking is a good way to break old patterns and establish new ones.

S=Specific – Inform your children of what specific behavior was not warranted, and then inform them of the desired behavior. Give examples of what the ideal behavior should be. Provide realistic potential consequences that could occur in their future (use the internet, books, literature, tours, etc.) to provide visual evidence of how others have been impacted by the same poor decision-making.

M=Moral – Inform your children of the morals that are learned from not engaging in negative behavior. Help them understand the meaningful purpose of their lives in respect to portraying positive behavior in the future. Explain to them how good morals impact the family as a whole and why good morals are important to the family's belief system. This moral stance should be repeatedly mentioned throughout the length of the punishment or reprimand. It should not only be spoken of during the initial confrontation; it should be used as a regular point of conversation in everyday life.

A=Attainable – This is where parenting is "turned up." You must make manageable punishments, ones that require little to no supervision once set. Consider the mental and social limitations that will impact your children and how they will eventually impact you. Avoid giving reprimands that need a lot of supervision from others, as this diminishes your ultimate authority when others don't carry it out fully. The punishment should be manageable by you for the entirety of its timeframe.

R=Realistic – Make the punishment or consequence realistic. Sometimes, out of anger and frustration, parents give out unrealistic punishments. When unrealistic punishments are given children tend to increase their level of defiance, which increases the parents' blood pressure. When attempting to implement the S.M.A.R.T. tool, base your consequences on social norms, peer age groups, and parenting resources. Seek counsel from a therapist as a way to gain knowledge on different ways to discipline particular age groups.

T=Time-limited – You should always give a timetable for punishments and consequences. When children are subjected to consequences that have open-ended timeframes (no end date) the punishment no longer seems to appear as a punishment. The punishment holds no value because the desire for the privilege tends to fade away. It is essential to reiterate the missed moral that caused the punishment, and to set an end date, to allow children the opportunity to gain back trust by showing an understanding of the moral. It is imperative when creating effective parenting strategies that you put timetables on each punishment or reprimand and STICK TO IT!

Not sticking to rules and showing moments of weakness in parenting (ultimately poor leadership skills) is a primary factor for children repeating undesired behaviors. Many children fail to learn the morals that parents desire for their children due to the parents' inconsistency in following through on the punishments and consequences. Basically, not following and applying the rules. For example, a sign of parenting weakness is when a parent says "it doesn't matter" or shows a lack of concern when the child begins to use the parent's phone although the child's own phone was taken away because of negative behaviors. This sends mixed messages to the child, the main one being that the parent really wasn't that upset, and the morals that the parent was speaking of were simply "crap."

Dating is another area that requires parent-child communication and sound rules and consequences. Millennial parents must understand that youth today consider dating as doing everything except literally going out together one on one. Talking on the phone extensively, spending time with each other at school, and having sexual relations can all be considered dating. Parents should explain to their children that it is okay for them to go out with the opposite sex as long as they are with others in a group setting, stressing that once in the group setting, they are NOT allowed to be alone, one on one.

The millennials' social movement has altered their way of thinking. They believe that because they are speaking daily on the phone and at school with someone they are infatuated with that they are officially dating. They never take into consideration that neither of them can drive or go off and be together exclusively without the permission and supervision of an adult. Many parents attempt to deny their children the right to even speak to the opposite sex outside of school. Informing children that they are forbidden to socialize with the opposite sex ultimately leads to sneaking and manipulative behaviors in a child's attempt to keep up with their social movement. The reality is that their hormones are jumping and racing, so attempting to deny them the basic experience of socializing with the opposite sex is simply unrealistic.

Parents need to embrace their children's growth, including puberty. They are encouraged to continue setting rules and boundaries related to dating, but not rules that are simply unrealistic. Parents who allow their children to entertain the opposite sex in the confines of their home have an opportunity to help "parent" the young man or young lady their child is interested in. Many times, parents can become a positive influence on other people's children by allowing them to have another place where they can come and get guidance in the form of structure and boundaries. When dating, a good rule of thumb is to allow younger teens (up to age 14) to go on group dates where they can enjoy being around their person of interest as well as family and friends. This way, the family and friends get to weigh in on the demeanor, attitude, and character of the person of interest. This is a good way to help guide teenagers on how to have healthy relationships with the opposite sex.

Once the children have turned 15, they should be offered the opportunity to obtain a driving permit. This is to ensure that they are capable and comfortable by age 16, when they are eligible to obtain a driver's license. This process is important for dating because during age 15, while working on the permit, teenagers should continue with group dating, allowing the family to have an opportunity to help guide them into picking relationship interests that are complimentary to them. At 16 years old teenagers should be able to obtain their driver's license and become comfortable with driving themselves. At this point-one-on one dating may begin. Now, teenagers should be responsible enough to drive themselves home or to a safe area if feeling threatened during the one-on-one date. Establishing guidelines related to dating can help children grow into their responsibilities and "rites of passage" timely and safely.

Action Brings Change

Every action of your life touches on some chord that will vibrate in eternity.
Edwin Hubbel Chapin

The family mission represents a CHANGE has come. No more of the "same ol' same ol'" because it is time for a new start. It means that the family members are "somebody" and that they stand together for a cause. The mission is different for every family, but every family needs to be on a mission. The mission chosen will represent how the family will survive many years to come; it will be the source of the legacies they leave for future generations. The mission sets the foundation for the state of survival of the family members mentally, physically, spiritually, emotionally, and financially. When families begin to take responsibility for their unit and become accountable for their children, then our society will benefit from the various positive views of a diverse world. Having a mission represents strength, rules, expectation, structure, and growth, all of which become inevitable to the family unit as a whole.

My Story

Allow me to share one of my personal family visions. We, my husband and I, wanted to live debt-free. We are both young African Americans who were raised in the inner city. Our mindset was fitting for the norms of the young people of our culture—work, and then spend with no savings in sight. We had gotten locked in with pawn shops and loan companies for small amounts, $100 here or $250 there. The overall sum of the accounts appeared to be insurmountable. Our attitude was Why pay it off? We did not understand the financial hold we were under due to how poorly educated by our parents we both were about spending and saving money. Yes, I am going to say "our parents" because they are who we should have learned the benefits of saving and spending wisely from. Neither my father (who raised me) nor did my husband's mother (who raised him) took the time to show us how to spend, save, or invest. Our parents made their money and spent it. They saved it as they saw necessary and that was it, never once taking us in and sitting us down to explain or educate us on ways to get ahead in life financially. My father's favorite saying was, "Don't ask, don't borrow, and don't beg…If you can't buy it yourself, you don't need it." I would get so annoyed when I would hear him speak this, mainly because it was his version of "no," meaning I had to find another way to get what I wanted or needed. The problem is my father had no input on where or how to save or invest my money. I pretty much was on my own, learning from friends and associates, which basically meant getting burned and messed over.

Due to my ignorance of how to obtain financial wealth and the lack of education from my parents, I co-signed on a car loan for someone I thought was my "best friend." I got stuck with the bill while she was driving another car because she wrecked the one I co-signed for, and placed it into bankruptcy court. She was free and clear to go to another car lot and purchase another car, while I was left with the bill to pay on the first car and a negative mark on my credit report.

My husband had similar issues related to saving and spending. We decided that life has to be better than paying pawn shops and loan companies. We thought about traveling and enjoying life knowing that our money was growing. We thought about preparing for what we could give our child that our parents didn't or couldn't give us or teach us. How could we be better than our parents in certain areas of our life? At that moment, in that conversation, our mindsets had changed. We no longer viewed our relationship with money as "easy come easy go." We began to get smart. We started to educate ourselves and to budget, sacrifice, and commit ourselves to the goal of eliminating revolving debt and saving our money.

The first thing we did was to sit down together and literally write out every bill we could think of. It didn't matter how small or how large the bill was; it went on the list. The next thing we did was to decide which bills could be paid off the quickest and planned to do just that. It didn't take just two months. In fact, it took more than seven months, but we stayed committed to the plan. As the months passed we were able to continue to add more bills to the paid-off list and remove them from the due list. Some bills required us to break them up in cycles. Some required we pay as little as $25.00 a month. Our plan was to not be overwhelmed by the bill collector because we were the ones in control due to understanding our mission, and having a family vision to erase debt. Having that mindset made us feel powerful when collectors called or when I called them to make arrangements, no matter how rude or insulting the collections agents were. Month after month, we saw our recurring bills decrease and become obsolete. The vision was coming to fruition and our mindset related to our relationship with money was changed forever. Now, our daughter will be raised better than we were when it comes to understanding finances. We had just begun to leave her a legacy of financial wealth.

Part III

Putting Your Plan into Action

Family Meeting Guide

You don't choose your family. They are God's gift to you, as you are to them.
Desmond Tutu

Before your first family meeting, visit http://www.dsga.pw/worksheet/ to download your Parenting Worksheet. The worksheet will help you frame your ideas on what parenting means to you, making it easier to explain the family vision and purpose of the family unit when you hold your family meetings.

1. Hold weekly meetings at the same time on the same day of the week to establish order in the family unit. Make this a priority. Members may be resistant at first because this is new and uncomfortable. Just remember being uncomfortable brings success, so insist they attend. If you remain consistent with holding the meetings, eliminating the distractions, and being positive, the family members will eventually conform.

2. You will initially conceive the topics. The topics are based on what morals and values you want instilled in the next generation, including traditions of the past, present, and future. If your family is a blended one, new traditions need to be formed. Having new traditions can help reduce anxiety and feelings of sadness connected with changes in the family structure.

3. Limit meetings to 20 minutes (Walton-McCawley & Walton, 2009, 17-20), never to exceed (note: when meetings exceed 20 minutes family members tend to disagree and disconnect). Someone always demands the attention and the opportunity will surely arise to exceed the time limit if you don't remain focused on the vision. Use a cooking timer (avoid using cell phones or gadgets) and designate a different person to keep time each week. The more the children are involved the more likely they are to participate.

4. Alternate roles by allowing family members to randomly pick a topic of discussion for the week's meeting related to the family's values, morals, or traditions. This way, everyone will feel equal in the decision-making. The

goal is to bring the family together; involving each family member with roles helps keep them attentive and engaged.

5. Eliminate any and all distractions during meeting time (turn off phones, etc.). Remind the family this is a family-mission gathering; hence no one is to speak disrespectfully of another under any circumstances. It is also a secret gathering. Nothing said by any family member is to be repeated outside of the family meeting time. This practice will help avoid accidentally saying something in front of the Naysayers and Why-ers.

   There is no room for negative energy during the meeting. The purpose of the meeting is to uplift and remind each other of the family's goals. You may have to literally confiscate electronic devices such as cell phones and tablets prior to the meeting to ensure there are no distractions.

6. Each family member must oblige family meeting rules, which are agreed on by all family members. Everyone gets to vote and the majority wins for each decision related to the family during the meeting. For example, if a family member is opposed to eating food during the designated meeting time, the family will discuss it as a whole, and then vote on whether eating will be allowed during future meetings. If the majority of the family agrees to no eating, the rule is to be respected by all members at all meetings, out of respect for the family unit.

7. Record the family meetings in a notebook to reflect on the growth and accomplishments that the family is making. Having positive reflections can lift the family's spirits in the midst of hard times and make the more triumphant times even more joyous. It is important to track accomplishments of the family as a whole as well as the efforts of individuals in the family who are working on the mission. Keep track by monthly viewing the progress level the family is making based on the actions that were assigned to them.

8. Commit to the process and remain consistent.

Happy Meeting!

Family Vision Guide

Vision is the art of seeing what is invisible to others.
Jonathan Swift

This vision is an example of a family whose vision is to end the generational poverty cycle in their family. But, it can be adapted to any vision a family has. Notice the vision is written. The goals are clear and reachable for this family unit of three, and steps are taken weekly to ensure action.

Vision: For family to become financially secure/wealthy in three to five years
Mission (Goal): End generational poverty for the Macker Family
Who makes up this family? (Important: do not focus on all relatives residing in the home. Only focus on the ones that you, as the parent, are RESPONSIBLE for.) Mom, 16-year-old daughter, and 9-year-old-son (NOT grandmother, auntie, and two cousins, even if they have the same last name and same home address).

Input

What are each family member's thoughts related to the vision and the mission?
Mom – positive thoughts (How can this vision help the family long-term?)
Mom – negative thoughts (How has the family been impacted when the vision was not there? Think of behavior patterns that had negative consequences due to lack of vision)
Sixteen-year-old daughter – positive thoughts (How can this vision help the family long-term?)
Sixteen-year-old daughter – negative thoughts (Question children to get their thoughts related to the lack of family vision and how corporate marketing and social media have influenced their thoughts related to family.)
Nine-year-old son – positive thoughts (How can this vision help the family

long-term?)
Nine-year-old son – negative thoughts (Question children to get their thoughts related to the lack of family vision and how corporate marketing and social media have influenced their thoughts related to family.

GOALS

Mother points out her goal to end generational poverty. She explains how ending generational poverty is in alignment with her values of abundance, assertiveness, leadership, growth, and determination. She is clear and specific with the children on the objectives to complete the goals. She has identified steps for each family member to take in order to complete their goals by their desired dates. Mother explains to her family that they will start saving and eating in for the next six months to accomplish their goal by the end of the year.

1. She explains the outcome of the goal
2. She makes objectives specific, measurable, attainable, realistic, and time-limited (Remember the S.M.A.R.T. system discussed previously can apply to any process, not just making rules and punishments.)

Action – Take It Slow

There are many things to consider when taking action because it requires actually doing something. It goes beyond writing, talking, planning, etc. Action should be taken in a step-by-step process to avoid feeling overwhelmed or feeling as if your end goals are hopeless. At this point, it is crucial to be mindful that you will receive gratification later; it will be delayed due to the long-term outcome that is envisioned and the consistent hard work that is now necessary. The new mindset the parent has is now ALIVE and is going to bring about change.

You should log your family's action by days or weeks and also by the months. At the end of every day or at the end of every week, or simply pick a day of the week that works best for the family members to sit together and think of their accomplishments related to taking action. Write them down. Title the paper [Action Taken and The Date]. This will help all family members SEE their vision coming to past. Each phone call, every new book read with the purpose of learning another way to protect the family's money needs to be written down. The old saying "out of sight, out of mind" is crucial to remember during this step of the vision. The less we see what we dream about in our daily lives, the more we forget about our dreams, which leaves us feeling frustrated, unappreciated, and overwhelmed.

Every so often, you must reflect on what has been accomplished in your lives as a whole. Your family should celebrate what has been accomplished no matter how minor the accomplishment. All of your family members should understand that when you celebrate you don't have to go on a shopping spree. You can celebrate with a group hug with all the family members, bake a cake with the children, take longer to leave the park, or simply stand in a circle and pat each other on the back (the circle of gratitude).

When Setting Rules and Consequences...

Children should have enough freedom to be themselves - once they've learned the rules.
Anna Quindlen

1. When dealing with a child who has had numerous encounters with school authorities, and maybe local authorities, too, and who remains unfazed and continues defiant behaviors, THERE IS STILL HOPE! It will require you forget the current age of that child and remember when the child was two years of age. You must then begin extreme parenting. Meaning, when the child is at home, they must be treated like a two-year-old. The child can no longer roam freely throughout the home, but must be guided and led. For example: if you are cooking dinner, the child should have to sit at the kitchen table until you are finished, or get up and help you. If the child wants to use the bathroom or get something out of the refrigerator, then the child must obtain permission. If the child wants to watch television, then you must approve that as well. Basically, you have to remind the child that they were given the freedom to walk about through the home and to do as they please, but that is no longer their right until their behavior is corrected. This takes dedication and commitment from you, but you must guide every move for the child. You only get a break from this lifestyle once the child is asleep or at school. Other than that, your entire mental energy must be focused on caring for a two-year-old again. Keep in mind that if the child continues unruly behaviors, being treated like a two-year-old will be the least of their problems in the youth detention center.
2. Practice unscheduled pop-ups at your children's school(s). Prepare yourself to do impromptu bus rides with you children. A child who misbehaves on a regular basis at school is more than likely very familiar with your daily routines. They become accustomed to your stating that you are unavailable due to work or other obligations and use it to their advantage when they want to misbehave. Taking time out to purposefully surprise your child at

school or to start volunteering may help reduce silent lunches, hearings, and other forms of school discipline that are the result of inappropriate at-school behaviors.

3. When millennial parents are introducing rules, limits, and boundaries to children they should have the children paraphrase what is being stated to them. This is a way to help decrease anxiety over not being sure of what the rule meant and a way to avoid statements later such as, "I thought you meant…" from children.
4. Be aware of how you approach your children when attempting to have them acknowledge their undesired behaviors. Be mentally aware not to confront children in a hostile manner, but in a positive one. Give clues to help children develop insight on the morals or values that were missed when the undesired behavior was displayed, but try to avoid verbalizing the actual behavior or telling children what they have done is disrespectful or disobedient. Having children verbalize their wrong behavior allows them to develop emotions related to their actions and to accept responsibility for their actions, as opposed to allowing the child to minimize, deny, or rationalize the undesired behavior. Once children are able to verbalize their wrongdoing, the rule, and the consequence, then both parties are clear as to what is happening and what the next step to move forward is. If a child is unable to verbalize their wrongdoing, rules, and/or consequences you must continue to move forward as planned with the rule and consequence(s) as they were originally stated. The key in establishing rules and order in the family unit when raising young millennials is to be consistent. This does require more patience and time when children aren't willing to accept responsibility for their actions, but it is your responsibility to remain consistent with following through on the rules, regardless of a child's defiance.
5. You must set your cell phone down and avoid using social media yourself in the presence of your child to model the desired behavior you wish your children to display. Just think about how many times your children have asked you a question, but you were staring at your phone and had to have

them repeat the question. At that moment you were parenting, teaching your children that you were not cognitively aware of them because at that time your mind was on the gadget. Be aware of their presence to avoid teaching undesired behaviors subliminally.

6. Arriving home from a busy day, you are ready to relax and not be bothered. Those are the times you have a higher risk of becoming agitated with active children or to avoid engaging with older children. It is a good rule of thumb to allow yourself and your children 20 to 30 minutes alone time once entering into the house. This will give each family member an opportunity to gather their thoughts related to family and forget the life that was just left outside the door (work, school, friends, traffic, etc.). The importance of this rule is to provide structure on how the family enters the house. Decrease the anxiety of feeling bombarded with concerns and problems as soon as you enter into your kingdom.
7. You can structure your children's 20 to 30 minutes to help them understand and appreciate the process by instructing children to place their school items in a designated area and immediately use the bathroom and wash their hands. Next, become comfortable in relaxed clothing and grab a snack. After that, find a location that is appealing to them, whether it is the couch or the dining room table, and sit and simply enjoy their snack. After the snack is finished, continue on to completing homework and chores.
8. Having a Pocket Wallet and a Savings Wallet/Carry Purse and a Savings Purse are habits that millennial parents need to adopt. Parents who are used to giving allowance or money to their children for rewards and "just because" should try implementing a savings structure to educate their children on the importance of financially taking care of "self" first. A pocket wallet or carry purse is what children keep in their possession. The savings wallet or savings purse is kept in your possession for the child. The savings monies can be transferred to a bank account if desired. When children are given money for any reason, a portion should be divided between the pocket and savings wallet/purse. When a special occasion or designated

event arises the children should be encouraged to use their pocket wallet or carry purse to purchase things for others and themselves (presents, gifts, birthdays, etc.). You will have to do your due diligence of saving the monies that are given for the savings wallet or purse. It is imperative that the rule is followed through once established. Children who earn money should learn how to manage their monies. They should also learn what it takes to manage finances for their current household. This will require spending quality time with your children to help them develop an appreciation of managing their income while being realistic with the cost of living. If your child contributes to the household's finances, but you never take the time to explain why the bill constantly increases or why the rate remains the same, the child will not appreciate the value of budgeting their finances. This will ultimately corrupt their ability to manage finances successfully in their early 20's and 30's.

9. Let's talk about rules and technology. Your children, from toddlers to teenagers, should have a limit on when they can engage with electronics like cell phones, computers, mp3 players, iPads, etc. It is a parent's right to set limits and boundaries on such items. Here are five limits that can be set on technology.
    I. Saturday and Sunday morning for three hours
    II. Monday through Friday children can be allowed two hours
    III. No contacts in cell phone unless you are aware of who the contact is
    IV. All social apps must be approved by you – meaning you are fully aware of the app and who it was ideally designed for (you should have the exact same app on your phone so you can learn it with proficiency)
    V. Chat accounts can only be visited in your presence (such sites as Kik, Snapchat, etc.). You should take time to insist that the child sit with you and get on the chat accounts so you can see how they are handling bullying and peer pressure from social media.

Many parents would love to forget about social media due to the negative influences it exposes their children to. Hopefully, sooner than later, millennial parents will embrace the fact that social media is here to stay and plays a vital role in the rearing of our children. Here are eight tips to embrace social media.

I. Know the rules. Use the internet and educate yourself on the various social apps that are available to children. Question your children to see what apps they frequent the most or what apps their friends frequent. These are the apps you should definitely familiarize yourself with. Make yourself aware of age restrictions, and share those restrictions with your children.

II. Be specific. Spell out the rules to children, making sure they understand your feelings and concerns related to the identified social apps.

III. Verbalize to your children the importance of not befriending strangers online. You should be the first to explain the dangers of online predators and verbalize to your children the safety reasons for only connecting with people online that they know in real life.

IV. Explain the consequences of social media by explaining that every post and every piece of information shared online will literally last a lifetime and can come back to haunt them. A good way to inform them is to remind them to think of you prior to posting or logging on. Tell children to ask, "Will this make my parent upset with me?" Or a good rule to follow is to have children evaluate themselves by thinking of how they would feel if their entire classroom saw the post. Is it something they would be proud to say, "I did it"? If not, it's probably not a good thing to share online.

V. Hang out in the background on social sites that your children visit. You should "follow" or "friend" your children to track their online activity. You must question your children about fake accounts and assure them that there is no need for fake accounts due to the dangers and risks fake accounts pose. You have the right to insist on knowing your children's user names and passwords.

VI. **Avoid being an overly active friend online, though, as you don't want to risk publicly embarrassing your children by commenting on their pages often. Remember, this is their social site, not another way to talk to your children. Save your comments for face-to-face dialect. You want to build unity in the family and talking through gadgets can too often encourage ways to disconnect.

VII. Keep an open door of communication with your children. Encourage your children to come to you about being bullied or if some activity they see just feels wrong, inappropriate, or uncomfortable. Ask your children to tell you of a conversation on social media that made them feel uneasy. Encourage them to talk about these moments because, the reality is, they happen. It happens to adults so it has to be happening to children. Suggest your children come to you with any questions regarding questionable messages or friend requests they receive from people they don't know.

VIII. Enforce the rules. Stick to them. If a child breaks a rule that has been set, then you must follow through with the consequences you had clearly laid out beforehand (e.g., shutting down an account, taking away their mobile phone for a week, etc.). If you are not able to follow the rules you discussed and agreed on, then the child is not likely to comply when you are attempting to parent, due to lack of leadership, trust, and clarity of values.

10. Avoid verbally threatening your children with punishments or reprimands. This practice devalues your authority over time. Millennial children need consistent guidance that entails rules and structure.
11. Be mindful that setting rules and consequences will change as your children grow older and as the social times change. Disciplining children is an ongoing progress until they are no longer their parents' legal responsibility.
12. Take time to listen to your children when setting consequences. Allow them to speak and truly attempt to understand their needs and wants in connection with the undesired behavior. You do not necessarily have to agree with the

children on the thoughts they have, but the mere fact that they are allowed to share helps reduce their anxiety related to feelings disconnected from you during a time of disappointing behavior.

Responsibility

In order to set family responsibilities for children, parents must be realistic concerning the cognitive and physical abilities of their children. Cindy Walton-McCawley and Kathleen A. Walton (2009) provide a list of capabilities for children from ages two and up. Although this is not their exact list, the principle is the same—age-appropriate chores for all children in the household (p. 17-20). Children should not be expected to do more than they are able, but they can each do something to help make the home they live in clean and comfortable for the entire family.

If the child is 8 yrs old then common responsibilities should include:

a. Assist with cleaning kitchen
b. Fold towels and put away
c. Bathe independently
d. Pick clothing for next school day
e. Draw pictures of gratitude for love ones with words of encouragement
f. Clean up after self (picking up their clothing and toys and placing them in appropriate areas)

If the child is 9 yrs old then common responsibilities should include:

a. Wash dishes with assistance
b. Fix prepared meals (heat in the microwave)
c. Clean bathroom with supervision
d. Fold own clothing plus towels and put all away in proper places
e. Take out trash with minimal direction
f. Dressing self for school and outings appropriately (matching, ironed, clean)

If the child is between the ages of 10 -14 yrs old the common responsibilities should include:

a. Clean room without being directed
b. Groom body and hair appropriately with minimal assistance (note: guidance is needed during puberty)
c. Mow lawn without assistance
d. Earn money for odd jobs / Develop saving ethics and moral for self worth
e. Cook side dishes or full meals for siblings or one dish for family gatherings
f. Take out trash and complete other chores without being prompted
g. Complete homework and turn it in on time without assistance or supervision
h. At this age children should be allowed to socialize with the opposite sex in a group gathering in which they stay in the group and do not venture off (such as at the bowling alley, movies, state fair, etc.)

For teenagers between the ages of 15-16 yrs old, common responsibilities should include:

a. Obtain driving permit
b. Investigate colleges, armed services, trade school, options for future
c. Seek possible part-time employment
d. Complete their laundry without assistance
e. Maintain passing grades in school
f. Complete chores without being prompted
g. *16-year-olds should be responsible enough to begin one-on-one dating

For young adults between the ages of 17-18 yrs old, common responsibilities should include:

a. Obtain driver's license
b. Verbalize plans for after high school and take action (make appointments for recruiters, college interviews, etc.)
c. Continue to clean after self in home (maintaining a clean room, helping in household chores, cleaning bathroom used in home, etc.)
d. Work a part-time job
e. Complete high school education / Obtain GED
f. Complete own laundry
g. Begin to contribute to household bills
h. Cook full meals for siblings and parents
i. Date

WORKSHEET

The Mirror

"We have to confront ourselves. Do we like what we see in the mirror? And according to our light, according to our understanding, according to our courage, we will have to say yea or nah-

and rise."

-Maya Angelou

What I Like about Me

What I want to Change about Me

This what I can physically, mentally, spiritually, and emotionally do to change me into the person I desire to be

Repeat the following line several times. Let this become your daily affirmation:

One life I must live, not just exist. Being a parent is my choice and my reward.

Definition of a Parent

Directions:

"PARENT," using each letter in the word parent, brainstorm characteristics and traits that a person must possess in order to parent successfully. Think of the generational social movement when you think of characteristics of the person.

P ______________________________

A ______________________________

R ______________________________

E ______________________________

N ______________________________

T ______________________________

***Now looking at the words that were written, how might "Parent" be defined?**

____

____

____

____

____

____

____

Resources

AT&T (2006). Do you speak teen? Advertisement.

(2015). Retrieved March 21, 2016, from http://www.merriam-webster.com/dictionary/mission

Carver, G. W. (n.d.). BrainyQuote.com. Retrieved March 21, 2016, from http://www.brainyquote.com/quotes/quotes/g/georgewash158551.html

Cave, N. (n.d.). BrainyQuote.com. Retrieved March 21, 2016, from http://www.brainyquote.com/quotes/quotes/n/nickcave547214.html

Chapin, E. H. (n.d.). BrainyQuote.com. Retrieved March 21, 2016, from http://www.brainyquote.com/quotes/quotes/e/edwinhubbe120545.html

Corporate Marketing. What is Corporate Marketing? (2012). Retrieved March 21, 2016, from http://www.marketing-schools.org/types-of-marketing/corporate-marketing.html

Covey, S. (n.d.). BrainyQuote.com. Retrieved March 21, 2016, from http://www.brainyquote.com/quotes/quotes/s/stephencov636510.html

Cuncic, A. (2016, February 27). What Is Aggressive Communication? Retrieved March 20, 2016, from http://socialanxietydisorder.about.com/od/glossarya/g/aggressive.htm

Dalai Lama. (n.d.). BrainyQuote.com. Retrieved March 21, 2016, from http://www.brainyquote.com/quotes/quotes/d/dalailama378036.html

Erikson's Stages of Development. (2016). Retrieved March 25, 2016, from http://www.learning-theories.com/eriksons-stages-of-development.html

Erik Erikson (2016). Wikipedia, the free encyclopedia. Retrieved April 4, 2016, from https://en.wikipedia.org/wiki/Erik_Erikson

Evans, S. J. (2015, October 22). Seven inmates given combined total of 20 YEARS in solitary confinement after making rap music video from their cells chanting 'I'm on fire' and posting it on WorldStar. Retrieved March 21, 2016, from http://www.dailymail.co.uk/news/article-3284187/Seven-inmates-given-combined-total-20-YEARS-solitary-confinement-making-prison-rap-music-video-posting-WorldStar.html

Fox, M. J. (n.d.). BrainyQuote.com. Retrieved March 21, 2016, from http://www.brainyquote.com/quotes/quotes/m/michaeljf189302.html

Gibbs, N. (n.d.). BrainyQuote.com. Retrieved March 21, 2016, from http://www.brainyquote.com/quotes/quotes/n/nancygibbs663146.html

Hull, J. D. (n.d.). BrainyQuote.com. Retrieved March 21, 2016, from http://www.brainyquote.com/quotes/quotes/j/janedhull224522.html

Kail, R.V. & Cavanaugh, J. C. (1996). Human Development. Pacific Grove, CA: Brooks/Cole Publishing Company.

Kik messenger app scrutinized following 13-year-old's death. (2016, February 3). Retrieved March 18, 2016, from http://www.cbsnews.com/news/kik-messenger-app-scrutinized-following-13-year-olds-death/

Meyer, P. J. (n.d.). BrainyQuote.com. Retrieved March 21, 2016, from http://www.brainyquote.com/quotes/quotes/p/pauljmeye190945.html

Motivational quotes and posters. First they will laugh. (n.d.). Retrieved March 21, 2016, from http://www.motivationblog.org/first-will-laugh/

Quindlen, A. (n.d.). BrainyQuote.com. Retrieved March 21, 2016, from http://www.brainyquote.com/quotes/quotes/a/annaquindl425725.html

Swift, J. (n.d.). BrainyQuote.com. Retrieved March 21, 2016, from http://www.brainyquote.com/quotes/quotes/j/jonathansw122246.html

Tutu, D. (n.d.). BrainyQuote.com. Retrieved March 21, 2016, from http://www.brainyquote.com/quotes/quotes/d/desmondtut112366.html

Urban Ventures. (2015). Facts About Poverty. Retrieved March 21, 2016, from http://urbanventures.org/facts-about-poverty

Walton-McCawley, C. & Walton, K. A. (2009). The Courageous Parent. Columbia, SC: Alderian Child Care Books Company.

About the Author

Glendora Dvine has been a nationally accredited licensed counselor since 2007. In 2010 she founded Dvine Systems GA, where she provides therapeutic and professional counseling services to families and individuals.

Glendora received her Master's in Psychology at South University in Savannah, Georgia in 2007. She was a trainer for Georgia's Commercial Sexual Exploitation of Children program in 2012. She has been a Certified Sex Offender Specialist since 2015, working with both juvenile sex offenders and sex crime victims. Since 2014, Glendora has been a speaker to audiences of parents, professionals, and children on topics that help them determine their vision and improve their communication patterns.

Glendora's passion for helping others can be heard and felt as she motivates, encourages, and inspires her audience to find their purpose in life and walk in it. Glendora is available to speak at companies, churches, and small organizations including local city and government entities.

Since 2011 Glendora has volunteered for the Wounded Warrior Program Give an Hour and at local public schools, encouraging healthy mental living, family safeguarding and reliable community connections.

Glendora now lives in McDonough, Georgia, with her husband of 16 years, Yaunte, and their 10-year-old daughter.

To book Glendora for your next event, please visit her website, http://www.dsgeorgia.com.

Made in the USA
Charleston, SC
23 April 2016